Unfiltered: The Political Life and Times of Matt Gaetz

Wilson Brain

Table of contents

Copyright

Dedication

About me

Introduction: Who is Matt Gaetz?

Chapter 1: Early Life and Family Legacy

Chapter 3: Matt Gaetz's Early Political Journey

Chapter 4: Loyalty in Action – Defending Trump Through Thick and Thin

Chapter 5: Controversies and Investigations – Navigating a Stormy Political Landscape

Chapter 6: Matt Gaetz and the Transformation of the Republican Party

Chapter 7: Controversies, Scandals, and Legal Challenges

Chapter 8: Gaetz's Political Legacy and Influence

Chapter 10: The Future of Matt Gaetz: Political Legacy and Prospects

Chapter 11: Matt Gaetz's Influence on the Republican Party and American Politics

Chapter 12: The Legal Challenges and Controversies Surrounding Matt Gaetz

Chapter 13: Matt Gaetz's Future: Political Aspirations and Legacy

Copyright

Dedication

"Unfiltered: The Political Life and Times of Matt Gaetz" delves into the complex and often polarizing journey of the Republican congressman. This book traces his political ascent, his steadfast backing of Donald Trump, and the legal hurdles he faces. It offers a thorough examination of Gaetz's impact on U.S. politics, his alignment with the populist movement, and the lasting influence he is creating in Washington.

About me

Wilson Brain is a political analyst and author who examines the careers and legacies of key American political figures. In "Unfiltered: The Political Life and Times of Matt Gaetz," Brain offers a thought-provoking look into the career of one of the most influential and controversial figures in U.S. politics today.

Introduction: Who is Matt Gaetz?

In the dynamic and often polarized world of American politics, few figures have garnered as much attention and stirred as much debate as Congressman Matt Gaetz. Representing Florida's First Congressional District, Gaetz has risen to prominence as one of the most outspoken members of the Republican Party. His political persona is marked by a combative stance, unwavering loyalty to former President Donald Trump, and a fierce commitment to challenging the traditional political establishment. To his supporters, Gaetz is a courageous patriot, willing to speak his mind and confront Washington's political elites. To his critics, he is a controversial figure whose actions often appear more provocative than productive, and whose political style blurs the lines of decorum.

Gaetz's political trajectory has been swift, propelled by a blend of ambition, a strong family legacy, and an astute use of media. His journey from a state legislator in Florida to a national figure has been anything but ordinary. Gaetz is not a typical politician; he comes from a well-connected family in Florida, yet he presents himself as an outsider. While he is a vocal advocate for law and order, he has also been the subject of significant scrutiny and controversy. These contradictions have led many to question not only who Matt Gaetz truly is but also what drives his unconventional and often divisive approach to governance.

Unfiltered: The Political Life and Times of Matt Gaetz seeks to delve into the man behind the headlines. Through an in-depth exploration of his early life, political career, and his role within the Republican Party, this book aims to provide a well-rounded perspective on a figure who has both captivated and outraged the American public. This book will present a nuanced portrait of Gaetz, analyzing both his achievements and the controversies that have defined his career.

As we journey through Gaetz's life and political rise, we will examine how his unique personality and principles have shaped his decision-making and alliances. Known for his confrontational style, Gaetz thrives in the media spotlight, skillfully using it to amplify his messages, rally his base, and provoke discussion. His command of social media, especially platforms like Twitter, has set him apart from many other politicians, allowing him to directly engage with his followers, respond to critics in real time, and shape the political conversation on his own terms.

At the same time, Gaetz's career has been marred by numerous high-profile controversies, including allegations of misconduct and investigations that have made national headlines. These events have only intensified the polarized opinions surrounding him, with his supporters often viewing these accusations as politically motivated attempts to undermine a leader who dares to challenge the status quo. For them, these controversies serve to reinforce his image as an outsider, unafraid to disrupt the established order in Washington, D.C.

To truly understand Matt Gaetz is to understand a critical moment in American politics. Gaetz is emblematic of a broader shift within the Republican Party—a move toward a more populist, anti-establishment conservatism that resonates with a significant portion of the electorate, frustrated with what they perceive as "politics as usual." Whether his influence will continue to grow or eventually fade, there is no denying the impact Gaetz has had on American political discourse. His story provides valuable insight not only into his personal journey but also into the larger forces that are reshaping the political landscape in the 21st century.

Unfiltered will explore the key moments that have defined Gaetz's career, delving into his most significant alliances and rivalries, and analyzing his impact on the Republican Party and American politics at large. Throughout this exploration, we will confront the complexities of a figure who defies easy categorization, whose political tactics have made him a lightning rod for both praise and criticism. No matter the opinion surrounding him, Gaetz remains a powerful and influential presence in Washington.

This is the story of Matt Gaetz—an individual who, regardless of public opinion, has remained steadfast in his beliefs and unwavering in his approach to politics.

Welcome to Unfiltered: The Political Life and Times of Matt Gaetz.

Chapter 1: Early Life and Family Legacy

1. A Legacy of Influence

Matt Gaetz was born on May 7, 1982, into a family deeply entrenched in politics, a backdrop that would greatly influence his future path. His father, Don Gaetz, made his mark on Florida politics as a state senator and former president of the Florida Senate. Growing up, Matt was exposed to the intricacies of political life, witnessing firsthand the responsibilities and influence that come with public service. This chapter examines how Matt's early exposure to the world of politics shaped his own ambitions and served as a catalyst for his career.

2. Hometown Values and Family Influence

Raised in the affluent community of Fort Walton Beach, Florida, Gaetz enjoyed a privileged childhood. His family's financial stability allowed him to attend prestigious schools, where he excelled academically and developed strong leadership skills through extracurricular activities. The values instilled by his parents—public service, community involvement, and a strong conservative foundation—became key elements of Gaetz's personal and political identity.

3. Don Gaetz: A Political Mentor

Matt's father, Don, played a crucial role in shaping his understanding of politics. As a respected and pragmatic figure in Florida's political scene, Don Gaetz was known for his commitment to conservative ideals and public service. This section explores Don Gaetz's career, including his work in healthcare reform and economic development, and highlights how his father's principles laid the groundwork for Matt's own political philosophy. Matt's father taught him the value of integrity in politics—an approach that would define his own career.

4. The Gaetz Family's Influence in Florida Politics

The Gaetz family has been a significant force in Florida politics, not only through Don Gaetz's career but also through their connections with other powerful figures in the Republican Party. This section delves into the political networks the Gaetz family cultivated, providing Matt with the support and connections necessary to launch his own political career. In this environment of influence, Matt learned early on the importance of relationships, strategy, and networking in achieving political success.

5. A Notable Ancestry

In addition to his father's direct influence, Gaetz's family history is rooted in public service, with ancestors who contributed to local government and law. This section briefly touches on Gaetz's family lineage, underscoring how the Gaetz family has been a steadfast presence in their community. This heritage gave Matt a strong sense of responsibility to uphold the family's legacy in public service.

6. Educational Foundations

Gaetz attended Niceville High School, where he showcased a natural talent for public speaking and debate. Known for his bold personality, Gaetz was not afraid to voice his opinions—traits that would later characterize his political career. After high school, he pursued a degree in political science at Florida State University, further honing his skills in argumentation and public discourse. He later attended the College of William & Mary Law School, where he expanded his understanding of constitutional law and policy, laying a solid foundation for his future political endeavors.

7. Early Encounters with Law and Ethics

During his time in law school, Gaetz faced the complexities of legal ethics, gaining valuable experience through internships at various law firms. This section explores his initial exposure to legal dilemmas and how these experiences shaped his understanding of integrity and ethics—lessons that would remain central to his career.

8. Shaping Political Ambitions

Gaetz's exposure to politics, combined with his education, led him to pursue a career in public office. Surrounded by influential mentors and community leaders, he began to develop his own ideas on governance, law, and justice. This section examines the early stages of Gaetz's political ambitions, highlighting how his background and education fueled his desire to enter politics and public service.

9. Lessons from a Politically Charged Upbringing

Growing up in a politically engaged family, Gaetz learned valuable lessons about the challenges and responsibilities of public service. This section discusses how his father's political career taught him the importance of resilience, handling public scrutiny, and the sacrifices inherent in public life—traits that would shape his approach to politics and define his persona in Washington, D.C.

10. Conclusion: Stepping Out of the Shadow

The chapter concludes with Gaetz's decision to enter the political arena and carve his own path, distinct from his father's legacy. Although he benefitted from his family's influence and connections, Gaetz was determined to create a political identity grounded in his own beliefs and bold style. His early life, shaped by family, education, and a strong political heritage, set the stage for his rise as one of the most controversial and influential figures in modern American politics.

Chapter 2: The Path to Politics

1. Early Career and Legal Education

After graduating with a law degree from the College of William & Mary, Matt Gaetz returned to Florida to begin his career in law. Armed with a solid legal foundation, he quickly realized his future lay not in the courtroom but in public service. Inspired by his father's legacy, Gaetz sought to make a difference in politics. This section delves into his initial legal career, the cases he worked on, and how these early experiences shaped his political perspectives, especially on issues like criminal justice and individual rights.

2. Entering Florida Politics: A New Political Voice

In 2010, Gaetz made his first significant political move by running for the Florida House of Representatives. His campaign was fueled by his youth, energy, and conservative vision. He campaigned on a platform centered around tax reform, smaller government, and public safety. The chapter explores his motivations, strategies, and how his family's network helped him gain early political traction. Gaetz quickly became a key figure within the Florida Republican Party, positioning himself as a voice for traditional values with a modern approach to governance.

3. Gaetz's First Term: Legislative Priorities and Key Issues

After winning his seat, Gaetz quickly made an impact in the Florida House. Known for his outspoken style, he championed conservative issues such as gun rights, taxes, and public health. One of his most notable stances was his support for Florida's Stand Your Ground law, which drew both praise and controversy. This section covers his key legislative initiatives and how his bold actions made him a standout figure in Florida politics.

4. Early Controversies and Political Opposition

As a new lawmaker, Gaetz encountered his fair share of criticism, particularly for his strong support of controversial policies like Stand Your Ground. His direct and combative approach to politics earned him both admiration and opposition. This section examines how Gaetz handled these challenges, maintaining his principles while navigating early political controversies.

5. Crafting a Political Persona: Media Strategy and Public Image

From the outset, Gaetz understood the role of media in modern politics. He built a recognizable public persona through frequent media appearances and a strong social media presence. Embracing platforms like Twitter, Gaetz engaged directly with voters, sharing his views and defending his stances. This section explores how Gaetz's media strategy helped him connect with younger, tech-savvy voters and solidified his place as a rising political star.

6. Lessons from the Florida Legislature

Gaetz's time in the Florida House was a period of rapid learning. This section highlights the political skills he developed, including how to navigate the legislative process, work with allies, and handle resistance. One of the key takeaways from his time in the Florida Legislature was the importance of persistence—something that would define his future in Congress.

7. Preparing for Congress

By the end of his time in the Florida House, Gaetz had built a loyal following and earned recognition as a leading conservative voice. Encouraged by his father and political allies, he set his sights on a Congressional seat in 2016. This section covers his decision to run for Congress, the challenges of his campaign, and how he utilized his reputation and media presence to win over voters.

8. The 2016 Campaign: Capitalizing on Trump's Momentum

During the 2016 election, Gaetz aligned himself with Donald Trump's populist message, which resonated with voters seeking change. This section details how Gaetz embraced the "America First" agenda and leveraged the growing political sentiment of the time to secure his

Congressional seat. His campaign was a reflection of his unwavering commitment to conservative values and his willingness to take on the political establishment.

9. Gaetz's Vision: A New Conservative Leadership

Upon entering Congress, Gaetz brought with him a fresh approach to conservatism—one that combined his media-savvy, unfiltered style with strong ideological conviction. This section outlines his goals as a new kind of conservative leader, one who was not afraid to challenge his party when necessary and represented the younger generation of conservatives.

10. Conclusion: A New Chapter in National Politics

The chapter concludes with Gaetz's swearing-in as a Congressman, marking the beginning of his national political journey.

His experiences in Florida politics had shaped him into a dynamic and resilient figure, ready to take on the challenges of Washington and continue his path as a bold and influential conservative leader.

Chapter 3: Matt Gaetz's Early Political Journey

1. Starting in Washington: Adjusting to the National Stage

When Matt Gaetz joined the U.S. House of Representatives in 2017, he quickly discovered the vast differences between state politics and the complexities of federal governance. This section covers his initial challenges, from understanding congressional procedures to navigating the influence of party leaders and special interest groups. Gaetz entered Congress during a politically charged time, with the Trump administration beginning to push forward its agenda. Energized by his success in Florida and his alignment with Trump's populist message, Gaetz entered Congress with a clear mission. This section highlights his early moves, including forging alliances, joining key committees, and adopting strategies to leave his mark.

2. Rallying Behind Trump: Becoming a Loyal Supporter

One of Gaetz's defining decisions was aligning himself as one of President Donald Trump's most vocal allies. From the start, he openly supported Trump, understanding that the president's populist agenda resonated with his Florida base. This section details how Gaetz's strong support for Trump shaped his policy views, public statements, and voting record. Whether defending Trump on issues like the Russia investigation or impeachment, Gaetz positioned himself as a defender of the president's agenda, using media and social platforms to amplify his loyalty. His alliance with Trump earned him prominence among conservative circles and helped cement his national political profile.

3. Media Savvy and Building a National Profile

Gaetz quickly emerged as a skilled media strategist. Unlike many of his colleagues, he used platforms like Twitter and appeared frequently on conservative news outlets, building his national presence. Known for his bold statements and controversial positions, Gaetz understood the value of media attention. This section explores how his provocative style drew both support and criticism, particularly from opponents who found his rhetoric divisive. Despite the risks, Gaetz's ability to generate attention played a key role in his rise, even as it led to backlash from political adversaries.

4. Key Legislative Stances and Policy Initiatives

Beyond his media presence, Gaetz took decisive positions on important legislative matters. This section covers his work on issues like immigration reform, regulatory rollback, and gun rights. Gaetz was particularly vocal in efforts to reduce government regulations and push for tax cuts. He also supported criminal justice reform, advocating for changes in the prison system and rehabilitation programs for nonviolent offenders. This section examines how Gaetz's mix of libertarian views and conservative values shaped his legislative work.

5. Defending Trump Amidst Investigations and Impeachment

The congressional investigations into the Trump administration, including the Russia probe and the impeachment inquiry, posed significant challenges for Gaetz. Rather than distancing himself, Gaetz became a staunch defender of Trump, viewing the investigations as partisan attacks. This section looks at his role in opposing the investigations, his public statements on conservative news networks, and his actions during the impeachment process, such as his protest during a closed-door deposition. Gaetz's steadfast support of Trump solidified his status as a key figure among the president's defenders, while further deepening political divisions.

6. Controversies and Ethics Complaints

Gaetz's time in Congress has not been without its controversies. This section delves into some of the most high-profile incidents, including allegations regarding campaign fund misuse and his relationships with lobbyists. Gaetz denied any wrongdoing, often dismissing criticism as politically motivated. His combative response to these controversies reinforced his reputation as a fighter against the political establishment, gaining him loyal followers but also creating significant opposition.

7. A Polarizing Force in Politics

By the end of his first term, Gaetz had become one of the most polarizing figures in American politics. His loyalty to Trump, media savvy, and willingness to engage in controversial debates endeared him to conservatives while alienating moderates and liberals. This section explores how Gaetz has embraced his role as a divisive figure, understanding that his appeal lies in representing the frustrations and values of his political base. Despite facing criticism, his ability to remain in the spotlight has solidified his place in the national political conversation.

8. Looking Ahead: Future Aspirations

The chapter concludes by examining Gaetz's future political ambitions. He has expressed a desire to continue shaping the Republican Party, pushing for a more populist and assertive direction. His relationship with Trump has positioned him as a potential future leader within the GOP. This section explores what lies ahead for Gaetz, whether within Congress or in higher political offices, suggesting that his career is far from over and that he will continue to play a key role in American politics.

Chapter 4: Loyalty in Action – Defending Trump Through Thick and Thin

1. The Rise of the Trump Loyalists

By 2018, Matt Gaetz had become one of President Donald Trump's most steadfast defenders in Congress. Unlike some Republican members who showed hesitance in supporting Trump, Gaetz fully embraced the president, positioning himself as a vocal and loyal ally. This section explores Gaetz's motivations for aligning himself so closely with Trump, revealing the strategic and ideological reasons that made this relationship central to his political persona. Gaetz saw Trump as not just a leader to support, but as a transformative figure who challenged the political establishment, aligning with Gaetz's own values.

2. Gaetz's Role in the Russia Investigation and Mueller Report

Gaetz's early test as a Trump supporter came during Special Counsel Robert Mueller's investigation into Russian interference in the 2016 election. Gaetz strongly opposed the inquiry, calling it a "witch hunt" and defending Trump during House debates and media appearances. This section details Gaetz's vocal opposition, including questioning the findings of Mueller's report, his attempts to discredit the investigation, and his use of social media to rally Trump's supporters. Gaetz's actions were bold and controversial, framing the investigation as a political attack rather than a legitimate inquiry.

3. Standing by Trump During Impeachment

Gaetz's loyalty to Trump became even more apparent during the impeachment hearings of 2019, which accused Trump of abusing his power by pressuring Ukraine to investigate political opponents. Gaetz vehemently opposed the proceedings, arguing that they were politically motivated and designed to weaken Trump ahead of the 2020 election. This section covers Gaetz's outspoken actions during the impeachment process, including his dramatic protest at a closed-door hearing, which he portrayed as a fight for transparency. Gaetz's defense of Trump solidified his image as a champion against what he viewed as a biased establishment.

4. Gaetz as a Media Presence: Amplifying Loyalty

Gaetz's media presence became a key part of his strategy to defend Trump. Unlike many politicians who limited their media engagements, Gaetz embraced every opportunity, particularly through conservative outlets like Fox News and Newsmax. This section examines Gaetz's media strategy, showing how he leveraged his platform to amplify Trump's message while presenting himself as a combative conservative. Gaetz's use of social media, particularly Twitter, allowed him to quickly respond to breaking news and shape narratives in favor of Trump, helping to solidify his image as a vocal supporter of the president.

5. Legal and Ethical Challenges

As Gaetz gained national attention for his loyalty to Trump, he faced increasing scrutiny, including legal and ethical allegations. Critics argued that Gaetz's unwavering support for Trump led him to cross ethical lines, including accusations of campaign fund misuse and violations of congressional rules. This section delves into the legal challenges Gaetz faced, discussing how he responded to these claims, often framing them as politically motivated. Despite the controversies, Gaetz's support from Trump's base remained strong, solidifying his position as a fearless defender of conservative values.

6. A National Profile: The Risks and Rewards of Loyalty

Gaetz's loyalty to Trump brought him national recognition and influence within the GOP, but it also made him a polarizing figure. His close alignment with Trump made him both a hero to Trump supporters and a target for critics. This section explores the dual nature of Gaetz's loyalty, highlighting how it elevated his profile while also subjecting him to intense scrutiny. Gaetz capitalized on this visibility, using it to further his conservative agenda while managing the political costs that came with his controversial stance.

7. Supporting Trump's Re-Election Campaign

As Trump sought re-election in 2020, Gaetz played a pivotal role in supporting the president's campaign. Gaetz viewed Trump's re-election as critical to advancing the policies he championed. This section outlines Gaetz's activities during the campaign, including participating in rallies, engaging with voters, and amplifying

Trump's message through the media. Gaetz's role in the campaign was more than symbolic; it demonstrated his deep commitment to continuing the conservative movement Trump had started.

8. Post-2020 Election: Loyalty Tested

After Trump's defeat in the 2020 election, Gaetz remained a staunch ally, questioning the legitimacy of the results and supporting Trump's claims of voter fraud. This section examines how Gaetz's unwavering loyalty to Trump during this time further deepened divisions within the Republican Party. Despite criticism from some Republicans, Gaetz continued to advocate for Trump, reinforcing his commitment to the former president's legacy and challenging the election outcome.

Chapter Summary

Chapter 4 illustrates how Gaetz's steadfast loyalty to Trump shaped his early career in Congress and solidified his influence within the GOP. His unwavering defense of Trump through investigations, impeachment, and the 2020 campaign marked him as a key figure in American politics. Despite facing legal and ethical challenges, Gaetz's loyalty brought both rewards and risks, enhancing his national profile while making him a highly controversial figure.

Chapter 5: Controversies and Investigations – Navigating a Stormy Political Landscape

1. Rising Profile, Intensified Scrutiny

As a staunch supporter of Donald Trump, Matt Gaetz quickly became a prominent figure in U.S. politics, attracting significant attention from both supporters and critics. His outspoken style and fearless approach to political issues brought him into the spotlight, placing him at the heart of multiple controversies. This chapter explores how Gaetz's increasing public visibility, combined with his combative political stance, drew intense scrutiny from the media, political adversaries, and even members of his own party. Gaetz's reputation for taking bold risks and his unwavering stance on divisive issues often created friction in Washington and beyond.

2. Personal Scandals and Allegations

A key controversy overshadowing Gaetz's political career involved a series of personal allegations, including accusations of unethical behavior and claims of misconduct. In 2021, reports emerged suggesting that Gaetz was under investigation for potential criminal activities, including possible links to trafficking laws and questionable financial dealings. This section details the unfolding allegations, the media's coverage, and Gaetz's vehement denials, along with his claims that the investigations were part of a politically motivated "smear campaign." Gaetz's response demonstrated his ability to frame himself as a target of the "deep state" and the "mainstream media," who he argued sought to destroy his career.

3. Navigating Legal and Political Fallout

As investigations into Gaetz's conduct progressed, he faced both legal and political hurdles that threatened his career. While some Republican colleagues distanced themselves, others offered support or chose to remain neutral, wary of alienating their own constituencies. Gaetz took a defiant stance, publicly denying any wrongdoing and casting the investigation as an effort to silence him due to his alignment with Trump and his outspoken conservative views. This section examines Gaetz's tactics during this challenging period, highlighting his strategic use of media appearances and social media to maintain his innocence and engage his base, despite the serious accusations he faced.

4. Gaetz's Defense: Framing the Scandals as a "Witch Hunt"

In his defense, Gaetz adopted a rhetoric similar to that of Trump, portraying the investigations as a "witch hunt" designed to bring down a political figure challenging the status quo. Gaetz insisted that the investigation was politically motivated, aiming to silence his conservative voice because of his close ties to Trump and his role as a disruptive force in Washington. This section analyzes the impact of Gaetz's "witch hunt" narrative, showing how he rallied his supporters and attempted to discredit the investigations as part of a broader attack on conservatives. His narrative resonated with a portion of the

Republican base who saw Gaetz as a victim of media and government overreach.

5. Public Perception and Media Coverage

Gaetz's controversies dominated the media, with coverage frequently portraying him as a divisive and embattled figure. His actions and statements only fueled the media's interest, keeping him in the public eye and sparking debates across news platforms, talk shows, and social media. While some viewed Gaetz as a reckless politician entangled in scandal, others saw him as a courageous figure standing up against a biased system. This section explores how the media shaped public opinion, detailing the contrasting reactions from conservative, moderate, and liberal commentators. Gaetz's frequent appearances on conservative news outlets helped solidify his base, even as mainstream media outlets continued to scrutinize his actions.

6. Support from Conservative Figures and Trump's Base

Amidst the scandals, Gaetz received strong backing from conservative figures, activists, and Trump loyalists who believed the controversies were part of a politically motivated attack. His strong connection to Trump proved beneficial as he gained endorsements from prominent conservative voices, some of whom argued that Gaetz was being unfairly targeted for his outspoken positions and efforts to hold the government accountable. This section examines how Gaetz used these endorsements to bolster his image as a victim of political persecution. His refusal to apologize or retreat from his positions only deepened his bond with Trump's supporters, who admired his resilience and willingness to challenge the political system.

7. Impact on Gaetz's Political Future

Despite retaining a loyal following, Gaetz's future in Congress became uncertain. Some Republican leaders viewed the controversies as a liability, while others feared that distancing themselves could alienate Trump-aligned voters. Gaetz's situation forced his party to navigate a delicate balance between supporting a popular figure and managing the reputational risks associated with his scandals. This section analyzes how these controversies may affect Gaetz's political future, including his prospects for re-election, influence within the party, and legislative power. For Gaetz, the scandals represented a critical moment that tested both his political resilience and the strength of his conservative base.

8. A New Path Forward – Lessons and Reflections

The chapter concludes by reflecting on the broader lessons from Gaetz's experience with scandal and controversy. His ability to withstand the pressure of accusations demonstrated his unwavering commitment to his brand of politics, marked by defiance, loyalty, and a readiness to challenge the political establishment. However, the chapter also considers the long-term effects of such controversies on a political career, acknowledging both the risks and rewards of operating outside traditional political boundaries. For Gaetz, the scandals were a dual challenge and opportunity, solidifying his standing with Trump's supporters while forcing him to navigate the realities of a polarized political environment.

In summary, Chapter 5 delves into the controversies that shaped Matt Gaetz's political career, exploring the complexities of his role as a defender of conservative values and a polarizing figure in American politics. Through his handling of scandals and investigations, Gaetz demonstrated both the strength of his convictions and the consequences of a confrontational political strategy. As Gaetz continues to face these challenges, he sets a new precedent for the kind of conservative leader willing to take risks and endure criticism in pursuit of a bold political vision.

Chapter 6: Matt Gaetz and the Transformation of the Republican Party

1. The Evolving Republican Party

Matt Gaetz's rise to prominence occurred during a pivotal time for the Republican Party. Following Donald Trump's election, the GOP shifted from traditional conservatism to a more populist, nationalist direction, with a heightened opposition to the political establishment. As a strong Trump supporter, Gaetz quickly became a key voice in this transformation, challenging both Democrats and Republicans who were not fully aligned with Trump's vision. This section explores the Republican Party's evolution during the Trump era and Gaetz's role within this change.

2. The Rise of Populism and Anti-Establishment Sentiment

A central element of Gaetz's political success was his embrace of populism. Like Trump, Gaetz positioned himself as an outsider, criticizing the "swamp" of Washington and the failures of traditional politicians. This section examines how Gaetz adopted populist rhetoric to strengthen his political influence, portraying himself as a defender of everyday Americans against the elite. His attacks on career politicians and the media resonated with a significant portion of the Republican base, aligning Gaetz with the "America First" movement, which sought policies to appeal directly to working-class Americans and Trump's supporters.

3. Gaetz and the Trump Doctrine

Gaetz's partnership with Donald Trump was a major influence on his career, both personally and politically. As one of Trump's most loyal defenders, Gaetz mirrored the president's combative style and consistently supported Trump's policies. This section explores how Gaetz embraced Trump's positions on issues like immigration, trade, and foreign policy, making him a key advocate for a new Republican ideology that prioritized national interests over traditional conservatism. It also discusses Gaetz's role in defending Trump during impeachment and investigations.

4. A Voice for the Far Right

Gaetz's alignment with Trump also led to his adoption by the far-right wing of American politics. As his rhetoric became more radical, he took increasingly extreme positions on issues like immigration, gun rights, and government power. This section explores how Gaetz's views resonated with far-right groups and conservative media, earning him widespread support within the

GOP's most radical factions. His willingness to challenge political correctness and engage in cultural conflicts made him a polarizing figure, alienating more moderate Republicans.

5. Gaetz vs. the GOP Establishment

Gaetz's rise was met with resistance, particularly from within his own party. The Republican Party was divided over how to handle Trump's legacy and the future of the GOP. While Gaetz remained a staunch supporter of Trump, many established Republicans sought to distance themselves from his influence. This section focuses on the internal struggles within the GOP, particularly the tension between Trump's populist supporters, like Gaetz, and the more traditional, establishment wing. Gaetz's combative style and aggressive tactics positioned him at the forefront of this ideological battle.

6. Gaetz and the Culture Wars

As the GOP shifted, cultural issues gained greater importance, with Gaetz emerging as a leading figure in debates over race, gender, education, and free speech. This section examines Gaetz's outspoken positions on issues like critical race theory, the Second Amendment, and immigration. His defense of traditional values and strong opposition to progressive movements made him a key figure in the GOP's culture wars, appealing to voters concerned with the left's cultural influence.

7. The Power of Social Media in Gaetz's Political Influence

In the era of social media, Matt Gaetz has expertly used platforms like Twitter and Instagram to amplify his political message. This section discusses how Gaetz bypassed traditional media outlets and built a grassroots following by engaging directly with his supporters. His use of social media allowed him to remain relevant, posting controversial opinions and calling out critics, thus strengthening his influence within the GOP.

8. Gaetz's Impact on Republican Policy and Legislation

Matt Gaetz has also played an active role in shaping GOP policy, particularly in foreign relations, defense, and law enforcement. This section explores Gaetz's legislative contributions, including his advocacy for a tougher stance on China, cuts to foreign aid, and stronger measures to combat illegal immigration. His policy efforts reflect his populist, America First ideology and demonstrate his influence on the GOP's agenda.

9. The Future of Matt Gaetz and the Republican Party

As Gaetz navigates a changing political landscape, his future within the Republican Party is uncertain. This section explores Gaetz's potential trajectory, considering his relationship with Trump, controversies, and the evolving dynamics of American politics. It asks whether Gaetz will continue to lead the populist wing or face challenges from emerging voices within the GOP.

10. Conclusion: Gaetz's Legacy in the GOP

The chapter concludes by reflecting on Matt Gaetz's lasting impact on the Republican Party. Gaetz has become a symbol of the new wave of conservative populism, defined by a strong opposition to the political establishment and media, as well as his steadfast support of Trump's agenda. Whether or not Gaetz remains a central figure, his influence on the party's direction during a critical time in American politics is undeniable. His role in shaping key issues, such as cultural conflicts and immigration policy, has solidified his place in the modern GOP.

Chapter 7: Controversies, Scandals, and Legal Challenges

1. Early Signs of Controversy

Matt Gaetz's political career has been marked by a series of controversies from the outset. Known for his bold rhetoric and willingness to challenge the status quo, Gaetz frequently found himself at odds with both his political adversaries and even moderate members of his own party. This chapter explores the early controversies that shaped Gaetz's career, beginning with his provocative statements and his ability to leverage controversy to rally his supporters. His unapologetic opposition to certain investigations and his alignment with Trump's rhetoric made him a polarizing figure long before more serious allegations emerged.

2. Gaetz and the Florida State Legislature

Before his time in Congress, Gaetz served in the Florida State Legislature, where his combative, no-holds-barred approach to politics first gained attention. As a state legislator, Gaetz took strong stances on various issues, including healthcare, gun rights, and deregulation. However, his confrontational style often overshadowed his policy work, setting the stage for the national political trajectory that would follow. This section reflects on his early career in the state legislature and the controversies that foreshadowed his later scandals.

3. The First Major Scandal: The Alleged Sexual Misconduct Investigation

In 2021, Gaetz became the subject of an investigation by the U.S. Department of Justice over alleged involvement in a sex trafficking scheme. Reports suggested that

Gaetz may have paid for sex with women, some of whom were underage. The scandal sent shockwaves through his career, leading to public scrutiny and media attention. Gaetz denied all allegations, framing the investigation as a political attack. This section dives into the details of the investigation, its impact on his public image, and how Gaetz responded to the scandal.

4. Gaetz's Defense: A Battle Against Media and Political Rivals

In response to the investigation, Gaetz adopted a combative approach, often portraying himself as a victim of a political conspiracy. Drawing parallels with Trump's media battles, Gaetz pushed back against his critics, defending his innocence through interviews and media appearances. Despite the backlash, his strategy helped him maintain support from his base, though it alienated some within the Republican Party. This section examines Gaetz's media tactics and his ability to rally supporters, even in the face of intense legal pressure.

5. The Greenberg Connection: Implications for Gaetz's Reputation

Joel Greenberg, a former associate of Gaetz, played a key role in the scandal. Greenberg, facing charges related to sex trafficking, was reportedly involved in some of the activities under investigation. Despite Gaetz's efforts to distance himself from Greenberg, their association raised questions about his judgment. This section explores the impact of Gaetz's connection to Greenberg on his reputation and public image.

6. The Fallout: Impact on Gaetz's Political Career

The scandal affected Gaetz's political career, causing some within the Republican Party to distance themselves from him.

While he maintained strong support from his base, the ongoing investigation cast doubt on his political future. Despite calls for resignation and pressure from his party, Gaetz continued to project confidence, navigating the fallout from the scandal. This section explores the impact of the scandal on his career and his ability to retain his congressional seat.

7. The Ongoing Legal Battle
As of the writing of this book, Gaetz's legal troubles are ongoing. The investigation continues, and the possibility of criminal charges looms. This section provides an update on the latest developments, including the potential for trial and the continued public debate surrounding the case. Gaetz's legal battles continue to shape his political narrative.

8. Gaetz's Future Amid Scandals and Legal Uncertainty

The future of Gaetz's political career remains uncertain as the scandal continues to unfold. While his supporters remain loyal, the legal challenges and ongoing controversy may affect his ability to hold office or run for higher positions. This section explores the potential paths forward for Gaetz, considering the possibility of him retaining his seat or transitioning to a new phase in his career.

9. Conclusion: Gaetz's Political Survival and Public Image

In conclusion, Matt Gaetz's political survival amidst scandal and legal uncertainty is a testament to his media savvy and the loyalty of his supporters. His ability to maintain influence despite the controversy surrounding him has reshaped his public image. This section reflects on how Gaetz's defiance in the face of adversity may define

his legacy, both as a politician and a symbol
of the populist wing of the Republican Party.

Chapter 8: Gaetz's Political Legacy and Influence

1. Defining His Political Identity

Matt Gaetz has shaped his political identity through his bold, often combative stance, carving out a prominent place in the Republican Party. Known for his unwavering conservatism, deep loyalty to former President Donald Trump, and his dedication to his Florida district, Gaetz has consistently challenged both party norms and the political establishment. His approach mixes populism with strong ideological beliefs, positioning him as a leader in the far-right faction of the GOP.

Gaetz's appeal stems from his resistance to political conventions, from his passionate speeches to his visibility on conservative platforms. By positioning himself as a voice for the people, he has both succeeded and faced controversy. This section delves into how Gaetz's political identity was formed and how it has contributed to his rise and the challenges he faces.

His rise has been marked by open criticism of both Democrats and moderate Republicans, utilizing inflammatory rhetoric to energize his supporters. This strategy has shaped his brand, offering insight into how his identity was forged in the modern political environment.

2. Championing Conservative Ideals: A Look at Gaetz's Policy Stances

Matt Gaetz's political career has been defined by his steadfast advocacy for core conservative values. From fiscal policy to social issues, he has championed traditional conservative causes. His tenure in Washington has focused on key issues such as:

Fiscal Policy and Taxes: Gaetz advocates for tax cuts, reduced government spending, and a streamlined federal government. His support for deregulation and limited government appeals to his libertarian-leaning conservative supporters.

Second Amendment Rights: A strong defender of gun rights, Gaetz opposes any new restrictions on firearms, using his platform to uphold the constitutional right to bear arms.

Immigration and Border Security: Gaetz has taken a hardline stance on immigration, advocating for stringent border control and the construction of a border wall, aligning with nationalist elements within his party.

Healthcare and the ACA: Consistently critical of the Affordable Care Act, Gaetz calls for market-based solutions to reduce healthcare costs, opposing government-run programs.

Foreign Policy: Embracing an "America First" approach, Gaetz favors reduced U.S. involvement in foreign conflicts and prioritizes national interests over international entanglements.

These policy stances reflect his representation of the more populist, right-wing side of the Republican Party, and his media presence has allowed him to maintain influence amid ongoing controversies.

3. Gaetz's Relationship with the Trump Legacy

A defining aspect of Gaetz's career has been his steadfast loyalty to Donald Trump, which has shaped his rise and continued popularity in the GOP. Even as others distanced themselves, Gaetz maintained his alignment with Trump's policies and political strategies.

The Impeachment Trials: Gaetz was one of Trump's fiercest defenders during both impeachment proceedings, participating in hearings and challenging the validity of the charges.

The 2020 Election: Gaetz was a vocal advocate for Trump's unfounded claims of election fraud and supported efforts to overturn the 2020 results.

Post-Trump Politics: After Trump's presidency, Gaetz continued to champion his agenda, promoting Trump-aligned candidates and appearing at rallies to solidify his connection to Trump's populist movement.

Gaetz's unwavering support for Trump has solidified his standing as a key figure in the

GOP, with his political views deeply influenced by Trump's legacy.

4. The Gaetz Brand: Controversy, Media Presence, and Populism

Matt Gaetz has built his political brand on a foundation of controversy and populism, embracing a brash, unapologetic style that has resonated with conservative media outlets. He leverages platforms like Fox News and social media to communicate directly with his supporters, bypassing traditional media channels.

This section explores how Gaetz has used media to amplify his message, positioning himself as a champion of the people while challenging the political establishment. His populist approach, though divisive, has garnered a loyal following. Despite the backlash from critics, Gaetz's ability to maintain his influence reflects the power of his messaging.

5. A Divisive Figure: Supporters and Critics

Gaetz's career is marked by a stark division between his passionate supporters and vocal critics. His backers view him as a fearless defender of conservative values, while his detractors see him as a divisive figure undermining political discourse. Despite controversies and scandals, Gaetz has maintained significant influence within the GOP, largely due to his ability to mobilize supporters and present himself as a voice for the people.

This section examines how Gaetz's polarizing approach to politics has shaped his legacy and explores the dynamics between his supporters and critics.

6. The Future of Matt Gaetz in American Politics

As of now, Matt Gaetz's future in American politics remains uncertain. Despite ongoing controversies and legal issues, his political influence shows no signs of waning. This section looks at potential future paths for Gaetz, considering the possibility of him remaining in Congress, running for higher office, or focusing on media and advocacy work. Gaetz's ability to galvanize his base may help him maintain relevance in the GOP for years to come, even amidst legal and political challenges.

7. Conclusion: The Enduring Legacy of Matt Gaetz

Matt Gaetz's legacy in American politics is marked by his unapologetic populism, strong support for Donald Trump, and controversial political style. While the future is uncertain, Gaetz's influence within the Republican Party and his ability to shape the political landscape will continue to leave a lasting impact. His political journey, characterized by bold actions and unwavering beliefs, will define his place in history as a powerful and divisive figure in modern American politics.

Chapter 9: Controversies, Scandals, and Legal Challenges

Matt Gaetz's political journey has been marked by bold rhetoric, controversies, and legal issues. This chapter explores the scandals and investigations that have defined his public image and political trajectory.

1. Sex Trafficking Allegations

In 2021, Gaetz was investigated for alleged involvement in sex trafficking, including accusations of paying for sex with a minor. He denied all allegations, calling the investigation a politically motivated smear campaign. His public defense, especially on conservative media, became a key part of his narrative, although the case's outcome remains unresolved.

2. Public Feuds and Provocative Statements

Known for his combative style, Gaetz frequently clashed with political opponents, including Republicans who criticized Donald Trump. His provocative comments, often on social media, sparked controversy and criticism, further solidifying his status as a political outsider and rallying his base.

3. Campaign Finance Investigations
Gaetz faced scrutiny over possible campaign finance violations, including improper expenditures. Though he denied wrongdoing, these allegations raised questions about his financial ethics and added another layer of controversy to his already tumultuous career.

4. Instagram Live Incident
In 2021, Gaetz appeared in a viral Instagram Live video with fellow lawmakers, joking about sensitive topics. The incident drew backlash, further highlighting his

unorthodox political style and lack of decorum, fueling calls for his resignation.

5. Resilience and the Future
Despite the legal and public challenges, Gaetz's resilience has solidified his reputation as a defiant political figure. However, his political future remains uncertain, as ongoing investigations and controversies continue to shape his career.

Conclusion:
Matt Gaetz's career is a blend of controversy and resilience. As investigations continue, his future in politics is unclear, but his bold, unapologetic approach ensures that he remains a prominent and polarizing figure in American politics.

Chapter 9: Controversies, Scandals, and Legal Challenges

Matt Gaetz's political career has been shaped not only by his outspoken, often polarizing rhetoric but also by a series of high-profile controversies and legal challenges. From accusations about his personal life to his involvement in contentious political moments, Gaetz has remained in the public eye. This chapter explores the major scandals and legal troubles that have influenced both his political path and public image, highlighting the ways in which Gaetz has navigated these challenges.

1. Sex Trafficking Allegations

The most significant controversy surrounding Matt Gaetz is the federal investigation into alleged sex trafficking. In

2021, the U.S. Department of Justice began looking into whether Gaetz had paid for sex with a 17-year-old, potentially breaching federal trafficking laws. Gaetz has denied the accusations, dismissing the investigation as a politically motivated attack and part of an extortion plot targeting his family.

The allegations were first reported by the New York Times in March 2021, triggering a media frenzy and leading to public calls for his resignation. Gaetz quickly rejected any wrongdoing, insisting that he was the victim of a smear campaign orchestrated by political rivals. Instead of staying silent, Gaetz took to conservative media, especially Fox News, to vigorously defend his innocence and challenge the legitimacy of the investigation. Despite his steadfast denial, the investigation has cast a shadow over his political future, with no final conclusions as of the latest updates.

2. Public Feuds and Provocative Statements

Gaetz's political style has often been confrontational, leading to numerous public feuds. His outspoken defense of former President Trump, particularly during the impeachment proceedings, put him at odds with some Republican colleagues, creating divisions within the party. Gaetz's media presence helped him cultivate a narrative of ideological purity, positioning himself against those he saw as too moderate.

His controversial comments have also drawn attention. Whether on topics like abortion, race relations, or the #MeToo movement, Gaetz has used provocative language to rally his base, even at the cost of stoking controversy. His combative approach on social media, particularly Twitter, has led to widespread backlash, though it has also solidified his image as an outsider unafraid to challenge the status quo.

3. Campaign Finance Concerns

In addition to the sex trafficking probe, Gaetz has faced scrutiny over his campaign finance practices. In 2021, reports emerged about questionable financial transactions involving his campaign, including expenditures that appeared unrelated to political activities. These allegations raised concerns about potential violations of campaign finance laws. Although Gaetz denied any misconduct, the attention on his financial dealings added another layer of controversy, threatening his image as a champion of the working class.

4. The Instagram Live Incident

In 2021, Gaetz faced backlash after participating in a casual Instagram Live video with fellow lawmakers, where they made inappropriate jokes. The video, which quickly went viral, sparked criticism from both Democrats and Republicans, who felt it reflected poorly on Gaetz's judgment. The incident led to calls for his resignation, with critics arguing that it demonstrated his disregard for the seriousness of the investigations into his conduct. Gaetz, however, remained unapologetic, viewing the incident as just another example of his unorthodox political approach.

5. Resilience and Future Prospects

Despite the numerous controversies, Gaetz has shown significant resilience. Throughout the investigations and public scrutiny, he has maintained his innocence and used his platform to rally support. For his followers, this defiance is seen as a sign of strength, portraying him as someone who refuses to be cowed by the establishment. However, the ongoing investigations leave his political future uncertain, and the ultimate impact of these scandals on his career remains to be seen.

Gaetz remains a divisive figure in American politics, with his future largely dependent on his ability to navigate the challenges ahead. His resilience and combative nature will likely continue to define his legacy, as the controversies surrounding him persist.

Conclusion of Chapter 9

Matt Gaetz's career has been marked by significant controversies, from legal challenges to public feuds and inflammatory remarks. His defiance in the face of scandal has earned him both fervent support and strong criticism. With investigations ongoing and new controversies emerging, Gaetz's future in politics remains uncertain. However, his unyielding stance ensures that his place in the political spotlight remains firmly intact for now.

Chapter 10: The Future of Matt Gaetz: Political Legacy and Prospects

As Matt Gaetz's career progresses amidst numerous controversies, legal challenges, and political struggles, his future in politics remains both unpredictable and intriguing. This chapter examines the potential outcomes for Gaetz, evaluating how his past actions might influence his political trajectory, the obstacles he faces, and how he could evolve as a political figure in the years to come. Will Gaetz be remembered as a hero of the populist right, a martyr for conservative ideals, or as a cautionary tale of political overreach?

1. The Impact of Controversies on His Political Future

Matt Gaetz's future is deeply tied to the controversies and scandals that have marked his career. From federal investigations into sex trafficking to scrutiny of his campaign finances, Gaetz has faced challenges that have derailed the careers of many. Yet, his defiant and unapologetic stance in the face of these allegations has set him apart. For his supporters, these controversies are seen as sacrifices made for challenging the political establishment, viewing him as a champion for truth in a corrupt system.

However, this defiance has also raised concerns among critics who question whether Gaetz's actions will ultimately lead to his downfall. With investigations still unresolved, Gaetz's political future remains uncertain. If he is cleared of wrongdoing, he may regain political strength and emerge with his reputation intact. However, any legal consequences could permanently tarnish his image, even among his most dedicated followers.

2. Gaetz's Relationship with the Republican Party

Gaetz has gained prominence within the far-right wing of the Republican Party due to his unwavering support for former President Donald Trump. His outspoken defense of Trump's policies and his frequent criticism of establishment Republicans have earned him a loyal following. However, his relationship with the broader GOP is complex. While he is supported by his base, more moderate Republicans view him as a disruptive force. If Gaetz's controversies continue to alienate swing voters and moderates, his long-term viability within the party may be questioned.

Nonetheless, Gaetz's strong alignment with the Trump agenda could solidify his influence within the Republican Party's populist wing. As the GOP redefines its identity in the post-Trump era, figures like Gaetz may become increasingly important. If the party continues to shift rightward, Gaetz could play a significant role in shaping policy and influencing the direction of the party.

3. The Influence of Social Media and Alternative Media Platforms

Matt Gaetz's rise to national prominence is closely tied to his strategic use of social media and platforms like Fox News. By utilizing these tools, Gaetz has effectively bypassed traditional media, communicating directly with his supporters and building a strong brand as a vocal critic of the political establishment. Social media platforms, especially Twitter and Instagram, have allowed Gaetz to stay connected with his base and control the narrative surrounding him.

However, this digital presence has its risks. The same platforms that help him reach supporters also amplify his critics. Gaetz's tendency to make provocative statements or engage in online disputes can alienate moderate voters and contribute to the divisiveness associated with his political style. His future will depend on his ability to balance his digital engagement with the need to appeal to a broader audience.

4. Potential for a National Political Role

Although Gaetz currently represents Florida's 1st Congressional District, speculation about his ambitions for higher office persists. He may one day seek a Senate seat or even the presidency. His public persona, centered on populism and loyalty to Trump, positions him as a potential national candidate, particularly within the conservative movement.

A Senate run could allow Gaetz to distance himself from local controversies and emerge as a national figure. His youth (born in 1982) means he could remain a prominent political figure for decades, potentially becoming a leader in a future conservative administration. His alignment with Trump's populist agenda could also benefit him if the Republican Party seeks a successor to Trump's political style.

5. The Role of Scandal in Shaping Gaetz's Political Identity

Gaetz's scandals and legal issues will play a crucial role in shaping his political legacy. While some politicians have used controversy to fuel their rise, others have seen their careers destroyed by it. Gaetz's future may depend on his ability to navigate these challenges, defend his reputation, and maintain the support of his base.

His combative nature suggests he could persist through adversity. However, as investigations into his conduct continue, the public's judgment of him will be critical. If cleared of accusations, Gaetz could strengthen his political standing. But if legal or political consequences arise, it may mark the end of his national political aspirations.

6. A Cautionary Tale or a Visionary Leader?

Ultimately, Matt Gaetz's future will be shaped by how history views him. Will he be remembered as a visionary leader who championed the conservative cause, defied the media establishment, and stood firm in the face of adversity? Or will he become a cautionary tale of ambition undone by scandal and self-destructive behavior?

For now, Gaetz's future is uncertain. His resilience has kept him in the spotlight, but whether he can convert his controversies into political victories or if they will lead to his downfall remains to be seen. His story is far from over, and his next steps will shape not just his career, but potentially the future of the Republican Party.

Conclusion of Chapter 10:

Matt Gaetz's political future is unpredictable but undeniably intriguing. As he navigates legal battles, party conflicts, and his public image, Gaetz remains a polarizing figure with the potential for both great success and significant failure. Whether he rises as a key leader in the conservative movement or fades into obscurity will depend on how he confronts the challenges ahead. His political legacy is still being written, with the next chapters likely determining his career and the future of the Republican Party.

Chapter 11: Matt Gaetz's Influence on the Republican Party and American Politics

Matt Gaetz's rise in American politics has become a reflection of the Republican Party's evolving dynamics. His outspoken style, consistent support for former President Donald Trump, and his challenges to the political establishment have made him both a controversial and significant figure. In this chapter, we explore Gaetz's impact on the Republican Party and the broader political landscape, analyzing how his actions and rhetoric continue to shape American politics.

1. Gaetz and the New Republican Populism

Matt Gaetz represents a shift within the Republican Party, one defined by populism, nationalism, and a strong alignment with Trump's rhetoric. Over the past few decades, the party has moved beyond traditional conservatism, evolving into a platform for populist sentiment that challenges established norms and political elites.

As one of the party's rising leaders, Gaetz embodies this change. His direct, unapologetic, and sometimes provocative style aligns with the populist wave that Trump popularized. His rhetoric speaks to the base of the party—working-class conservatives who feel overlooked by elites and the political establishment. Through his media appearances and social media presence, Gaetz has positioned himself as a key defender of this new Republican Party.

Gaetz's confrontational approach has garnered both support and criticism within the party. While some view him as a hero for challenging compromise and advocating for bold stances, others see his tactics as divisive. Despite this, Gaetz's influence on reshaping the party's direction is undeniable, as his style offers a model for future Republican leadership.

2. Gaetz's Challenges to the Republican Establishment

Matt Gaetz has consistently challenged the Republican establishment, opposing party leaders he deems too willing to compromise. His vocal criticism of figures like Speaker Kevin McCarthy has solidified his position as a leader of the party's most conservative faction.

Although Gaetz has been in office for multiple terms, he has built his career as an outsider, frequently confronting Republican leadership on issues like the COVID-19 relief packages and Trump's impeachment. His refusal to support Republican figures who did not fully align with Trump's agenda has earned him a loyal following among Trump-aligned conservatives but also sparked tension with more traditional Republicans. These divisions within the GOP highlight an ongoing battle between establishment Republicans and populist insurgents, with figures like Gaetz driving the conversation.

3. Gaetz and the "Culture War" Politics

Matt Gaetz has become a central figure in the Republican Party's embrace of "culture war" politics. Whether opposing COVID-19 lockdowns or challenging critical race theory in schools, Gaetz has aligned himself with the party's growing focus on cultural and social issues. This focus has become a defining part of the GOP's strategy, positioning the party as the defender of traditional American values against what they view as a radical left-wing agenda.

Gaetz's stance on cultural issues has helped him connect with his base, particularly on topics like education, free speech, and parental rights. His outspoken opposition to progressive policies on race, gender, and education has made him a key player in the culture war, rallying conservatives who feel threatened by left-wing ideologies. Gaetz's approach has proven successful, particularly in appealing to suburban parents concerned about their children's education and values.

4. The Gaetz Effect: Polarization and Partisan Loyalty

Matt Gaetz's rise has contributed to the growing political polarization in America. His style of politics, focused on division and partisanship, mirrors the tactics used by Trump, often fostering an "us versus them" mentality. Gaetz has become a polarizing figure, with supporters viewing him as a staunch defender of conservative values, while critics see him as a symbol of the divisiveness plaguing American politics.

The "Gaetz effect" reflects his strong influence on how Republicans view party loyalty, often demanding unwavering support on contentious issues like immigration, abortion, and the direction of the party itself. Gaetz's approach has further cemented his role as a key figure in the GOP, aligning him with the party's most loyal and vocal supporters.

5. The Future of Gaetz's Influence in American Politics

While Gaetz's future in American politics remains uncertain, his influence is likely to endure. As one of the most prominent figures in the populist movement, Gaetz will continue to shape the Republican Party's direction. Whether he stays in Congress or transitions to higher office, Gaetz's brand of populism and combative politics will remain a major influence on American politics.

Gaetz's ability to adapt to a post-Trump GOP will be critical to his long-term influence. As the Republican Party continues to evolve, Gaetz's role in shaping its future will remain pivotal. His journey, much like the future of the GOP, is still unfolding, and his impact on American politics will be felt for years to come.

Conclusion

Matt Gaetz's influence on the Republican Party and American politics is undeniable. From his role in shaping the party's populist wave to his embrace of culture war politics, Gaetz has been instrumental in reshaping the GOP. As the political landscape evolves, his future in American politics will continue to make waves. Gaetz's story is far from over, and his impact on the GOP and American politics will remain significant in the years ahead.

Chapter 12: The Legal Challenges and Controversies Surrounding Matt Gaetz

Matt Gaetz's political journey has been marked by numerous legal controversies. As a prominent figure, his actions, statements, and personal life have attracted intense scrutiny. This chapter explores the most significant legal challenges and scandals involving Gaetz, their impact on his career, and the lasting effects on his public image.

1. The Alleged Sex Trafficking and Corruption Investigation

In 2021, a major legal controversy emerged when the New York Times reported that

Gaetz was under federal investigation for sex trafficking involving a minor. This probe was part of a broader investigation into his associate, Joel Greenberg, leading to media frenzy and calls for Gaetz's resignation.

Gaetz was accused of engaging in illegal activities related to sex trafficking and public corruption. Greenberg, a former Seminole County official, had already pleaded guilty to sex trafficking, identity theft, and wire fraud charges. Investigators suggested that Gaetz might have been involved in a scheme involving the payment for sex and the transportation of women across state lines, in violation of federal laws.

Gaetz strongly denied the allegations, labeling them as false and part of an extortion plot. Although the investigation continued, no formal charges were filed, but the accusations damaged his reputation and raised questions about his credibility.

2. The Joel Greenberg Scandal

The sex trafficking investigation was closely linked to Joel Greenberg, Gaetz's former associate. Greenberg, indicted for several crimes, including trafficking minors for sex, wire fraud, and identity theft, was believed to have used his ties to Gaetz to facilitate illegal activities.

Greenberg's cooperation with authorities in exchange for a reduced sentence escalated the pressure on Gaetz. While Gaetz was not directly charged, his association with Greenberg fueled further criticism and added to his controversial image.

3. Ethics Investigations and Financial Misconduct

In addition to the trafficking allegations, Gaetz faced multiple ethics investigations over financial misconduct and potential misuse of his congressional office. In 2020, he was accused of soliciting campaign donations and favors from wealthy donors in exchange for political support, while also facing scrutiny for his extravagant lifestyle.

The House Ethics Committee investigated these claims, questioning whether Gaetz had violated congressional rules. While no major sanctions were imposed, the investigations intensified the negative perception surrounding him, reinforcing the view that he was pushing ethical boundaries.

4. Media Influence and Political Opposition

Media coverage played a significant role in shaping the narrative surrounding Gaetz's legal troubles. While some outlets, particularly conservative ones, defended him, others, especially those with a liberal stance, amplified the allegations. Gaetz used conservative media platforms to counter the accusations, presenting himself as a victim of a political attack.

Meanwhile, his political adversaries leveraged these controversies to challenge his credibility and weaken his influence. The combination of intense media scrutiny and political opposition created a volatile atmosphere, making every new development in the case significant.

5. Public Opinion and Political Consequences

The ongoing legal issues have had a profound impact on Gaetz's public standing. While some constituents continue to support him, believing the allegations are politically motivated, others have expressed concerns about his character. Despite his defiant stance, the accusations have polarized public opinion, with supporters viewing him as a fighter against the political establishment, and critics seeing him as a symbol of corruption.

6. The Future of Gaetz's Political Career

The future of Matt Gaetz's career remains uncertain. The legal battles and ethics investigations will likely continue to influence his political trajectory. If the allegations are disproven, Gaetz may recover politically, though the damage to his reputation could be long-lasting. If the legal challenges lead to criminal charges, it may mark the end of his career.

In any case, Gaetz's rise to political prominence, fueled by controversy, has made him a highly polarizing figure, and his future in politics will depend on how he navigates these ongoing legal and ethical challenges.

Conclusion of Chapter 12:

Matt Gaetz's legal controversies have been a defining feature of his career. Despite his denial of the accusations, these scandals have deeply affected his political standing. As Gaetz faces continued legal battles, his political future remains uncertain. How he handles these challenges will determine the next chapter of his career, but one thing is clear: his legacy will always be tied to the controversies surrounding him.

This version removes unnecessary repetition and tightens the focus on the key events and implications, aligning with Amazon's content guidelines.

Chapter 13: Matt Gaetz's Future: Political Aspirations and Legacy

As we reach the final chapter of Matt Gaetz's story, questions about his future and legacy in American politics remain prominent. Despite the controversies and legal issues that have often overshadowed his career, Gaetz continues to be a key player in the Republican Party and national politics. His loyal supporters and unapologetic political style suggest that he may remain influential in Washington, but his path forward will depend on key factors. This chapter explores the potential directions Gaetz could take in the future, the changing political climate, and how his legacy will be defined by his actions in and out of Congress.

1. Gaetz's Political Future: A Path Forward in Congress

Matt Gaetz's future in Congress will depend on his ability to overcome the complex political and legal challenges that have plagued him. Currently serving as the representative for Florida's 1st District, Gaetz enjoys a loyal voter base that appreciates his firm conservative positions and outspoken critique of the political establishment. However, ongoing legal investigations and public scrutiny could significantly impact his reelection chances.

The critical question for Gaetz is whether he can retain his seat in Congress despite the legal hurdles. If the investigations are resolved favorably, Gaetz may continue to build his political career, particularly if he aligns himself with the growing populist wing of the Republican Party. His supporters, who view him as a defender of conservative values and an opponent of the political elite, could support him in future elections, allowing him to maintain political power.

However, if legal issues lead to charges or convictions, Gaetz might face pressure to resign, effectively ending his congressional career. Even if no criminal charges are brought, the continued negative press and public scrutiny could damage his relationships with key donors and voters, diminishing his political influence.

2. The Rise of the Populist Wing and Gaetz's Role

Matt Gaetz has been a vocal ally of the populist wing within the Republican Party. Over time, he has positioned himself as a staunch defender of former President Donald Trump's policies, taking firm stances on issues such as immigration, taxes, and government spending. He has also criticized the Republican establishment, calling for a shift from traditional party politics toward a more combative, populist approach.

This alignment with the populist movement has made Gaetz a prominent figure among conservatives who feel disillusioned with the establishment. His support for Trump's "America First" agenda and his willingness to challenge the status quo have earned him a dedicated following. Should the populist faction continue to rise, Gaetz could become an even more influential figure in Congress, shaping policy and legislation that reflects his values. His combative style and dedication to his beliefs may also open doors for higher leadership positions within the party or a potential run for higher office.

3. Potential for a Run for Higher Office

Though Gaetz's future in Congress is uncertain, he may pursue higher office. Throughout his career, he has shown ambition, with speculation that he could run for Governor of Florida, a U.S. Senate seat, or even the presidency. His popularity among conservatives and his reputation as a fighter for right-wing causes could position him well for such a bid—if he can overcome the ongoing legal and ethical challenges.

A run for Governor of Florida would provide Gaetz with an opportunity to expand his influence, especially given the state's prominence in national politics. As governor, he could continue to champion conservative policies, potentially building a strong political foundation for a future national campaign.

Alternatively, Gaetz may aim for a Senate seat, either in Florida or another state, if an opportunity arises. With his outspoken nature and strong base of support, a Senate campaign could elevate his profile nationally and strengthen his influence within the Republican Party.

However, Gaetz's ambitions for higher office will be met with obstacles. Legal issues and public controversy could become major points of attack for opponents, making it difficult for Gaetz to gain broader appeal beyond his conservative base.

4. Gaetz's Influence on Republican Politics

No matter where his career leads, Matt Gaetz's influence within the Republican Party is undeniable. Despite the controversies surrounding him, Gaetz has become one of the most vocal and divisive figures in the GOP. His criticism of party leadership, unwavering support for Trump, and hardline positions on key issues have secured his place as a significant figure in the party's right-wing faction.

Gaetz's rise reflects the broader trends within the Republican Party, where populism has become more powerful in recent years. His use of media platforms, particularly conservative outlets like Fox News, has helped him maintain relevance and connect with voters. Whether he stays in Congress or moves to higher office, Gaetz's influence will likely continue to shape the party's future.

5. The Legacy of Matt Gaetz: Champion or Pariah?

As Gaetz's career continues to unfold, his legacy remains uncertain. Will he be remembered as a champion of conservative values—a politician who stood firm in the face of adversity? Or will he be seen as a pariah whose career was marred by scandal and controversy?

The answer to this question depends largely on how Gaetz handles the challenges ahead. If he emerges from his legal troubles unscathed, he could be seen as a key figure in the Republican Party's resurgence. However, if the allegations against him are proven true, his legacy may be overshadowed by scandal.

Regardless of how history judges him, Gaetz has already made a significant impact on the Republican Party and American politics. His rise to prominence and his unapologetic political style have cemented his place as a polarizing figure in the populist movement.

6. Conclusion: Matt Gaetz's Uncertain Future

As this book concludes, Matt Gaetz's future remains uncertain. Though he is a prominent figure in the Republican Party, his political career is far from secure. Legal battles and controversies continue to shape his journey, and it is impossible to predict what the future holds for him. What is clear is that Gaetz's influence on American politics will persist, whether through his continued role in Congress, a potential run for higher office, or his lasting impact on the Republican Party's direction.

Gaetz's story is far from over, and how he navigates the challenges ahead will determine not only his political future but also the legacy he leaves behind. The unfolding of his career serves as a case study in modern politics, where ambition, public service, and controversy are often intertwined, reshaping history in the process.